About the Author

LINDEL BARKER REVELL

Lindel Barker Revell is an Australian astrologer, clairvoyant, inventor and writer. Lindel has been working with the mystical tradition of the Tarot for self-discovery and prophecy for twenty-two years and practicing astrology for seventeen years.

Born in Hobart, Tasmania, Lindel moved to Sydney in 1974. Over the past five years Lindel has appeared in print media, on radio and television in Australia and the UK discussing the esoteric traditions of Tarot and astrology and the rising of interest in feminine values. She has a Masters degree in Applied Science (Social Ecology). In 1989 she co-invented the major astrological boardgame, *Revelation: The Game of the Future*, which was widely released in the UK. A firm believer in the power we each have to access our own intuition and wisdom, Lindel has taught many people the art of Tarot reading in a simple, individual way.

This book allows the reader to directly connect to the power of the spiritual symbols of the Tarot, the 22 Major Arcana cards. *The Tarot & You* is suitable for beginners and those with knowledge of the cards.

The Tarot & You

A simple guide to using the cards for self-discovery and prophecy

Lindel Barker Revell

Illustrated by Penny Lovelock

Contents

Introduction 6

What are Tarot Cards? 7

Ancient Origins and Modern Meaning 8

A World of Symbols and Archetypes 10

Astrology, the Four Elements, and the Suits of the Tarot 11

Open to Your Own Psychic Ability with Tarot 15

How to Use this Book for Divination 16

How to Separate the Major Arcana Cards 16

Getting in the Mood 16

Becoming Familiar with the Tarot 17

Shuffling 17

Asking a Question with a One Card Answer 18

Tarot Oracle 21

The Major Arcana — Upright and Reversed Divinations

0. The Fool 22

I. The Magician 26

II. The High Priestess 30

III. The Empress 34

IV. The Emperor 38

V. The Hierophant 42

VI. The Lovers 46

VII. The Chariot 50

VIII. Strength 54

IX. The Hermit 58

X. The Wheel of Fortune 62

XI. Justice 66

XII. The Hanged Man 70

XIII. Death 74

XIV. Temperance 78

XV. The Devil 82

XVI. The Tower 86

XVII. The Star 90

XVIII. The Moon 94

XIX. The Sun 98

XX. Judgement 102

XXI. The World 106

Alternative Spreads 110

Alternate Pathways (2 Card) Spread 110

Past, Present, Future (3 Card) Spread 110

Suggested Reading 111

Introduction

SHROUDED AS IT is in myth and superstition, the Tarot aroused mixed feelings in me when I first saw its vivid images. With trepidation I took out the instruction leaflet enclosed in the box of 78 cards and began what has become a journey of more than half my lifetime. In those days, books on how to read the Tarot were not readily available in the town where I lived, so I learned slowly through my own experience, only gradually coming to know the cards. It was over ten years before I picked up a well laid-out book which confirmed and expanded much of what I had learned on my own.

When faced with the task of writing a book on the Tarot, a great friend and guide to me, I wanted it to be simple enough even for the beginner yet thorough enough to impart some of its strength and wisdom. Students often find it difficult to learn the Major Arcana as the principles of these cards are quite complex. So while describing the structure of the whole Tarot pack, I concentrate on the 22 spiritual cards of the Major Arcana in a simple and direct way. The illustrations of the Major Arcana cards by Penny Lovelock provide a fresh interpretation of Tarot images and symbols that is excellent for divination and meditation.

What are Tarot Cards?

TAROT CARDS ARE the ancestors of modern playing cards. A full Tarot pack consists of 78 cards. Twenty-two of these are called the Major Arcana, or *Greater Secrets,* and contain the spiritual dimension. These were the original trump cards, the name coming from the word triumph. The remaining 56 cards are known as the Minor Arcana, or *Lesser Secrets.* They are divided into four suits, numbering one through ten, with a jack, knight, king and queen in each suit. The 56 cards of the Minor Arcana seem to refer to ordinary life with all its joys and hardships, while the court cards represent people encountered in everyday life. The four suits are wands, pentacles, swords and cups, which correspond to the four elements: fire, earth, air and water (see page 11). In modern playing cards these suits have become known as clubs, diamonds, spades and hearts. The combination of the two packs is thought to have happened in Italy in the fourteenth century.

The 22 Major Arcana cards along with four knights, one from each suit, are missing from our present form of playing cards. Of the 26 "lost" cards, only one has remained. The ancient Tarot Fool card has become our modern Joker and is generally not played, viewed with some suspicion, or even seen as an omen of bad luck.

A freeing up of attitudes in the twentieth century has enabled artists and psychics to create many fresh images of the Tarot. Of the Tarot packs designed this century, the most famous was created by Arthur Edward Waite and illustrated by Pamela Coleman Smith, both members of a British mystical group, *The Golden Dawn.* They took earlier more obscure images and made them more accessible, while adding in symbols of astrology and the Hebrew *Cabala. The Tarot and You* Major Arcana (see Tarot Oracle page 21), illustrated by Penny Lovelock, draws on much of the rich symbolism of the Waite deck, as well as other ancient and modern decks. Choosing a Tarot pack is a matter of personal preference. The cards depicted in *The Tarot and You* are devised as a pack for meditation and study as well as divination.

Ancient Origins & Modern Meaning

STRANGE YET FAMILIAR, the images of the Tarot haunt and entice, repel and invite. Where do they come from?

Veiled in the mists of time, the origin of the Tarot remains speculative. Scholars agree that the earliest playing cards, while not Tarot as we know it, originated in China and Korea, around the eleventh century. Some say Gypsies brought the Tarot to Europe from Egypt. While it does seem that the Gypsies held great secrets in the use of the Tarot for divination — the art of reading cards to predict future events — the cards themselves emerged for popular use in Europe in the fourteenth century. However, Gypsies were not known to be in Europe in any substantial numbers until the mid-fifteenth century. Other scholars suggest the Tarot was brought to Europe by Arabs from Northern Africa and Spain. Some time before the fourteenth century, Arab soldiers were to be found playing a card game called *naib*, which maybe derived from the Spanish word for cards, *naipes*. The Arabs may have brought cards with them, or perhaps this ancient knowledge was safeguarded by secret societies, such as the *Knights Templar* or the *Cathars* harking back to Babylon, and released for general usage during the Medieval Renaissance. In 1415, the famous Visconti deck was commissioned for the young Duke of Milan. It is still available today in a facsimile edition.

Condemned by the Roman Catholic church from the early fifteenth century but never entirely suppressed, the Tarot went through many changes in design. The oppressive Christian regime of the Middle Ages caused the Major Arcana to be shrouded in layers

of symbolic and allegorical imagery. Fortunately, the images could be understood by both scholars and ordinary folk used to street pageants enacting spiritual stories.

As the Dark Ages ended, people from many nations journeyed the Continent, and Europe experienced an enormous exchange of information and cultural growth. In some ways, this period of history can be seen to parallel our present information explosion. Historically, when established philosophies and stories falter in holding a society together, humans look to the ways people found guidance in the past in an attempt to fill the spiritual gap. The twentieth century, with its unprecedented wars, technological advances, and environmental catastrophes, has caused spiritual and religious beliefs to be questioned. Many people are turning inwards, or to other ways of viewing the world.

It is to the inner world that the Tarot belongs. Tarot images are recognized by Eastern and Western mystics alike to contain the great, universal symbols of the human spiritual journey. The Tarot connects easily and strongly with other mystical and esoteric traditions, such as the Hebrew *Cabala,* astrology, and numerology. The "New Age Movement" has unearthed many of the old wisdoms, from Runes to crystals. The Tarot has again emerged and with it, in its rich layers of imagery, ancient wisdom that time and many cultures have failed to suppress. The presence of the "Great Mother Goddess," for example, who is found in images of the Empress and High Priestess — also apparent in the figures of Justice and Strength, and in other cards where she appears as an angel — embodies ancient ideas of feminine power which were condemned in Medieval times and actively persecuted with witch-hunts and burnings.

Whatever their origin, Tarot cards continue to reveal themselves in each century afresh, because their system of symbols allows the mind to access and explore its hidden depths. Tarot is more accessible than, say, astrology or numerology, because it operates from the world of symbolic imagery and speaks directly to us through the visual. Tarot is a helpful tool for understanding yourself and others. Opening yourself to the inner world and building a relationship to that realm is essential for any real unfolding of the Tarot.

A World of Symbols & Archetypes

A symbol is an image, word, or object, a reference point that draws you through it to some deeper meaning. Religions employ symbolic language and images as a path to the spiritual. Symbols are interpreted differently by people with different belief systems.

> *As the mind explores the symbol, it is led to ideas that lie beyond the grasp of reason.*
>
> Carl G. Jung *Man and His Symbols*

Tarot images seem to come from the same unconscious source as dreams, the place where individuals spontaneously produce symbols. Certain meanings or associations have been established for Tarot images, yet each person will have an individual response to its symbols. Here lies the creative and dynamic aspect of Tarot. No matter how complex or obscure the symbol may be, the image is always meaningful. One of the great fascinations of symbolic images is the power they have to encode meaning, such as a dream that will not leave you or a Tarot image, like the Hanged Man, that is strange and haunting.

As recurrent motifs, archetypes have the ability to reproduce similar mythical ideas in the dreams or myths of individuals or whole communities. Archetypes are like seeds imbued with the latent power of life.

The Major Arcana contains archetypal images that bypass the rational mind. The Emperor can represent masculine power and hold further meanings of the Father archetype found in human memory, myths, and stories. Equally, the Empress evokes the power of nature and the Mother archetype. Like myths and dreams, Tarot cards have many layers of meaning. Study of their symbols will continue to reveal mysteries.

Astrology, the Four Elements, & the Suits of the Tarot

TAROT CARDS HAVE long been associated with astrology. Each of the Major Arcana cards used in this book has an astrological correspondence with an element as well as a planet or a sign. These connections are set out on page 14 as well as appearing with the description of each of the cards in The Tarot Oracle, see pages 22–109.

The four elements — fire, earth, air, and water — are the basis for the four suits of the Tarot — wands, pentacles, swords, and cups. The Ancients believed that all matter was made of combinations of these four elements. This idea has been recently revived by popular astrology, which describes the 12 zodiac signs according to the elements. A professional horoscope will delineate an individual's personal blend of elements in its various proportions. No one is all fire or water, but rather, a blend of the elements, similar to a Tarot reading.

Visual images of the four elements are also seen in many of the Major Arcana. For example, the four elements lie on the table before the Magician. Temperance and The Star card are seen balancing water with the other elements. The Tower shows the power of air and fire as thunder and lightning. The Justice card holds the sword of truth, associated with the element air. It is believed that when shuffling or "washing" Tarot cards the elemental components of them align in proportions which suit the individual and their concerns.

FIRE

Fire represents that which is hot, energetic, self-motivating, enthusiastic, upreaching, and competitive. It is the lightest of the elements, reaching up the highest, and has therefore become symbolically linked to the high aspirations and competition so valued by hierarchies and patriarchal societies. Fire consumes what surrounds it in order to burn more brightly. An alchemist of the sixteenth century, Paraclesus, noted that fire parallels life in that each must feed on other existence to stay alive. In the hearth it protects, warms, and transforms food by cooking. Out of control, fire consumes, destroys, blackens, and, at the same time, purifies.

In the Tarot, fire has become associated with the suit of wands. We describe people who display fiery characteristics as being warm, bright, and shining. Negative characteristics such as being domineering, tempestuous, or volatile are also fiery traits. The fire signs of the zodiac are Aries, Leo, and Sagittarius. Those born under these signs are said to be adventurous, exciting, born leaders, full of initiative, and courageous.

EARTH

Earth evokes that which can be depended upon. It is passive and nurturing, like our home the receiving earth and her rhythmic seasons. Earth is the heaviest of the elements, and as such, can have negative connotations, while at the same time representing the material world and its abudant wealth. This element may also be seen as something to be conquered plundered, and exploited until all resources are used. There is an inevitability about earth; we come from her and to her we return, ashes to ashes, dust to dust.

The pentacle cards, the earthy suit of the Tarot, have come to symbolize financial gains and losses, the way we earn our living, pursue a career, or acquire the steady wealth of land and houses. Solid and reliable, our concept of elemental earth pervades our language in figures of speech, such as "earthy," "down-to-earth," "solid as a rock," "safe as houses," "stick-in-the-mud," or "heavy-going." The earth signs of the zodiac are Taurus, Virgo, and Capricorn and are said to be practical, realistic, abundant, and loyal.

AIR

Air, vast and unseen, surrounds everything on earth. It is subtle, gives warmth and drafts, bubbles up, connects all things, and is changeable like the wind. Air in the form of breath has long been associated with our soul or spirit. In many ancient cultures it was thought essential to catch the last breath of a dying person in order to ensure reincarnation. The gesture made by the priestess who performed this ritual became known as the "kiss of death". "Inspire" and "expire" are words connected with this element. The Muse who inspires the musicians, poets, and other artists was said to materialize out of the air.

The Tarot suit associated with air is swords. In this suit the struggles and vicissitudes of life are shown. Air represents the realm of the mind. The power of thought which separates humans from animals is seen by the Tarot as being a two-edged sword. Rational thought is one of our greatest abilities, yet Tarot suggests achieving a balance between the head and the heart. The air signs of the zodiac are Gemini, Libra, and Aquarius. They are said to be clever, versatile, and intellectual in their skills and appreciation of the arts. On the other hand, people under the air sign can occasionally be "airy-fairy", "air-heads"; they may tend to "talk a lot of hot air" or "build castles in the air".

WATER

Water is symbolic of the fluid, deep, unknowable, renewing power of the emotions. Life-giving water dissolves, washes, cleanses, reflects, and promotes growth. The ocean is vast with unimaginable depths; the river is wide and seemingly calm yet hiding snags and dangers; a clear rock pool may teem with life. Water takes its shape from its container. As a destructive force, it overwhelms and drowns.

Cups is the Tarot suit associated with water. It has come to represent feelings, the family, and all matters to do with love and affection. The water signs of the zodiac are Cancer, Scorpio, and Pisces and are said to be loving, sensitive, emotional, musical, and tenacious. Descriptions such as "wet blanket", "drip", "as weak as water", or one's resolve "turns to water" have entered our language owing to the influence of this element.

Elemental & Astrological Associations of the Major Arcana

NUMBER	NAME OF CARD	ELEMENT	SIGN OR PLANET
0.	The Fool	Air	Uranus
I.	The Magician	Air/Earth	Mercury
II.	The High Priestess	Water	Moon
III.	The Empress	Earth/Air	Venus
IV.	The Emperor	Fire	Aries
V.	The Hierophant	Earth	Taurus
VI.	The Lovers	Air	Gemini
VII.	The Chariot	Water	Cancer
VIII.	Strength	Fire	Leo
IX.	The Hermit	Earth	Virgo
X.	The Wheel of Fortune	Fire/Water	Jupiter
XI.	Justice	Air	Libra
XII.	The Hanged Man	Water	Neptune
XIII.	Death	Water	Scorpio
XIV.	Temperance	Fire	Sagittarius
XV.	The Devil	Earth	Capricorn
XVI.	The Tower	Fire	Mars
XVII.	The Star	Air	Aquarius
XVIII.	The Moon	Water	Pisces
XIX.	The Sun	Fire	Sun
XX.	Judgement	Water	Pluto
XXI.	The World	Earth	Saturn

Open to Your Own Psychic Ability with Tarot

WE ALL HAVE psychic potential. Primal cultures acknowledge this in their attention to dreams, premonitions, and so on, while Western thought has tended to scoff at psychic intelligence, considering such matters unproven, unscientific, and therefore non-existent. As Westerners, we must leap cultural hurdles before we can listen to our intuition and allow it to work in and for us. If we have a strange feeling we think, "Oh, I'm imagining it," only to have those feelings later proved. Such feelings should be acknowledged. Vestiges of these feelings are known as "women's intuition."

The best way I know to become more psychic is to listen to your inner voice, and to record your thoughts and impressions in some way, such as a dream journal. This voice may come as a thought, an image, a dream, or a persistent daydream or feeling. Tarot cards, with their wealth of encoded symbolism, are excellent tools with which to awaken the mind to deeper knowledge. When looking at the cards, allow your mind to relax and soften your eyes to lose their sharp-edged focus. Parts of a chosen card may seem to float to the foreground, or you may fix on a certain symbol. In this way, elements emerge as important or significant.

Maggie, for example, while looking at The Sun card, became alerted to the red banner the child holds. All other details of the card stepped back from her softened vision. When asked what it reminded her of, she responded: "It's red, which feels energetic like blood racing through my body. If I take this road I will feel energy and life because it is linked to my life-force." Maggie saw this road was her own creativity through painting and she made the decision to return to her art. The weariness she had been experiencing fell away. Interestingly, The Sun card is traditionally associated with creative force, but it was her individual vision that gave her the impetus to do something practical in her own life.

How to Use this Book for Divination

The Tarot and You allows easy access to some of the ideas and symbols of the Tarot. Only the 22 Major Arcana cards are used, as these cards always contain the keys or openings into an individual's Tarot reading or "spread". The Major Arcana or *Greater Secrets* offer spiritual clues and guidance regarding the question you hold in your mind at the time. The Tarot Oracle (see pages 21—109) offers divinations for the cards in both the upright and reversed positions. You can use the Major Arcana from any pack of Tarot cards, or contemplate the Major Arcana that is specially illustrated in this book.

HOW TO SEPARATE THE MAJOR ARCANA

To use your own pack of 78 Tarot cards with this book, you need to separate the 22 Major Arcana from the Minor Arcana. The Major Arcana cards usually have their names written in capital letters at the bottom of the card and a Roman numeral from 0—XXI at the top of the card. You can check your cards against The Major Arcana listed in the Tarot Oracle on page 21.

GETTING IN THE MOOD

Consulting any oracle requires a calm, relaxed mind. Creating a special ritual for yourself can help to attain a mood in which you are open and receptive to the cards. Music, a candle, incense or essential oils all work on the emotional, etheric self, to calm and relax you. You may like to wrap your cards in a piece of natural fabric such as silk or cotton, or perhaps keep them in a wooden box. Traditionally, fabric used for this purpose is chosen with great care. The color and design should be particularly pleasing to you or somehow symbolic, such as choosing the color associated with your astrological sign. The act of unwrapping Tarot cards or taking them out of a box is in itself a ritual act. Do not leave your cards about for anyone to touch casually. Connecting to the Tarot is like building any relationship based on respect.

BECOMING FAMILIAR WITH THE TAROT

When you first look at the cards it is important to spread them out well, on a table or on the floor, so that all the images can be seen even if they are sideways or upside-down. Allow your eyes to casually wander over the images and rest here and there as if observing a landscape. With your mind free of questions, simply let color or design attract you, select the card you like *most* at the moment, then the one you like *least* or that is most disturbing. Make sure you pick up the card as you see it, whether in an upright or reversed position. Look up the meaning of the card in the Tarot Oracle on pages 22–109. These cards can reflect your mood of the moment, or even indicate your unconscious feelings regarding the cards.

SHUFFLING

Shuffling invokes a mystical power which links the handler to the ancient knowledge held within the cards. You will need a large, flat surface upon which to place the cards face-down. With your non-dominant hand — if right-handed, use your left — begin a circular, mixing or "washing" action, moving the cards around and amongst each other. When properly shuffled and dealt, it is believed that the elements of fire, air, earth, and water assemble in proportions that align with the inquirer's personal blend of elements. See Astrology, the Four Elements, and the Suits of the Tarot on page 11 for further explanation. Medieval thinkers believed this mingling of elements as

described by the Tarot suits reflected events in the outer world. These principles lie behind modern use of the Tarot as well.

ASKING A QUESTION WITH A ONE CARD ANSWER

The simplest and often the most direct way to consult the Major Arcana is to have a question in mind and to select one card only as your answer. Proceed to shuffle or "wash" the cards as described on page 17. A question may occur to you as you do this or you may have had a question when you first touched the cards. Allow this question to move in your mind as your hand circles and moves the pack. If you are left-handed, use your right hand or if right-handed, use your left to do the selecting.

Frame your questions in the following ways for best results:
"I need guidance in my relationship with X."
"What approach should I take at work?"
"How can I understand this time in my life?"

A rule of thumb is to keep the question very simple. General questions could be:
"What do I need to know at the moment?"
"What is the right action for me to take now?"

Do not ask questions requiring timing, such as:
"When will I find the one I love?"
"When will my finances improve?"
A better way to phrase your inquiry would be:
"I need guidance on finding the right relationship."
"What approach should I take to my finances?"
It is very difficult to become expert at divinations concerned with the timing of

events. Many professional readers refuse to attempt chronology for their clients because the world of symbols, myth, and Tarot operates with a different sense of timing from our world. Disconnect yourself from the modern addiction to time management and open yourself to the fluidity offered by the Tarot. The cards see questions as going through various phases and developments.

Each card represents a different and distinctive principle from the world of symbols. It has a title, a number, and an astrological association which all add to its meaning. The selected card does not offer a definitive truth or answer, but will offer you a way of viewing your question which expands the realm of possible outcomes. Cards also comment on your state of mind regarding the question. Whether you receive the card upright or reversed, you will find it helpful to read both the meanings and the description, as each reflects the other. A change in attitude may turn the card around as you decide to act in accordance to the knowledge you receive.

Ask the same question only once a day, and a maximum of three different questions on any one day. Asking the same question of the Tarot, without allowing enough time to contemplate its previous advice, will throw up disconnected and seemingly meaningless images. Reflect on what was revealed when you first asked your question and if you are not satisfied, ask again the next day. There will probably be a development in you regarding the question, especially if you give it some attention during the day. This might involve placing the answer card somewhere prominent so you can see it, or even meditating on its images.

For answers of more than one card, see Alternative Spreads on page 110.

Tarot Oracle

MAJOR ARCANA CARDS

0. The Fool

I. The Magician

II. The High Priestess

III. The Empress

IV. The Emperor

V. The Hierophant

VI. The Lovers

VII. The Chariot

VIII. Strength

IX. The Hermit

X. The Wheel Of Fortune

XI. Justice

XII. The Hanged Man

XIII. Death

XIV. Temperance

XV. The Devil

XVI. The Tower

XVII. The Star

XVIII. The Moon

XIX. The Sun

XX. Judgement

XXI. The World

0.

The Fool

RULING PLANET: URANUS

DESCRIPTION

An androgynous youth stands on the edge of a cliff, seemingly heedless of the drop below. The Fool represents our inner self about to embark upon another of life's adventures. A little white dog jumps at the heels of the youth, a symbol of our need to listen to our instincts. Held in the left hand is a white flower, which represents our essential purity. The youth carries a wooden staff or rod at the end of which is a bag or bundle representing the need to "travel light" in our new adventure. This bag is thought to hold the four magical symbols of the Tarot, the wand, the cup, the sword, and the pentacle. The whole figure of The Fool denotes openness, carefree joyfulness, and innocence.

0. The Fool

Upright Meaning

The Fool heralds a new cycle in your life. It is time to cast away the doubts and fears that often arise when leaving the well-trodden way; the known path. You stand poised between the old and the new and you will experience mixed feelings. The Fool in the Tarot guides you to step off the cliff of your old ways of thinking or acting and allow the journey to begin. Listen to your instincts in all matters regarding this new beginning and you will find you have a clear feeling about people and situations that need to be left behind. The little white dog which jumps along beside you will remind you with a bark or snap of intuition if you should go to make a wrong decision. The "silliness" of the Fool retains the ancient meaning of being particularly blessed when being absolutely yourself.

The change you are facing may happen suddenly, but upon reflection you will realize the opportunity has been right there in front of you for some time. This is both a challenging and exciting time. An important decision must be made, so be courageous and bold. Nothing new can come from staying at home and taking no risks. It may be time for you to re-enter life after a period of retreat or illness. In his bundle, the Fool has all the magical elements necessary for a new life: the cup, the pentacle, the sword carried on the rod or wand. The Fool's spirit is akin to your immortal

0. The Fool

Self, and the willingness to be a part of life and change. Remember that The Fool is a wise card which has its own special disruptive timing. Plans go awry. An adventure is in the air. In love, expect a new direction; in business, take a calculated risk; in all old or stale parts of your life, expect a shake-up and a bit of fun. Think matters through as best you can, then trust your feelings about what to do next. Steady yourself somewhere between natural fear and rashness and this card can take you anywhere.

Reversed Meaning

When you draw The Fool reversed you must be prepared to stop, look, and listen. You can become confused by too many details and miss the obvious. Remember, you are essentially free just like the Fool in the card and you do not have to dance to anyone's tune. However, do not rush into an opportunity which presents itself, for there may be unseen problems. It is almost as though there is a hidden snag as the fool steps off the cliff. Drawing The Fool card does indicate something inside you wants an adventure, a change, and this is a very real feeling. A change will come soon, but this opportunity may not be the right one, or something about it needs to be adjusted and made more safe. The warning is to keep a sense of reality and apply common sense to any new venture. Wait and sleep on it before giving your answer to anyone.

I.

The Magician

DESCRIPTION

The Magician stands behind a table on which are placed the symbols of the Tarot: the wand, the pentacle, the sword, and the golden cup. These symbols stand for the four magical elements of fire, earth, air, and water, which in turn correspond to creative intuition, practicality, thought, and emotion. The Magician holds his right hand up to heaven, and his left hand points to the earth, indicating the link between the two. Above his head is a figure eight, or *lemniscate*, the sign of infinity. This suggests the never-ending looping between our world and the unseen. He is the alchemist who transforms dross into gold. The Magician represents the power of the imagination, the mind and the ability to work with elemental forces.

I. The Magician

Upright Meaning

The Magician appears when you are about to use your mental power to imagine and create something new in your life. When you link to the power of The Magician, you blend with the force of life. This life force is ultimately potent and supremely creative. Like the Magician in the card, you may be faced with a choice of several very possible alternatives. The Magician is the archetype of the enormous power of your creativity when it is allowed to express itself. So, if faced with a choice at the moment, let your imagination run riot. Ask yourself: "What would happen if I did this and that together?" The Magician is able to blend different options to create something quite new which will work very well. Remember, water and earth are very different elements, but together they nourish each other and bring forth life. Do not limit yourself to old or set patterns of thinking about any problem at hand. Make lists of all your options and try to draw links between those you think are very different. This is not an either/or situation, or The Magician would not have appeared.

The Magician can also manifest in your life as the ability to help you to shine, perform, or market your abilities. This is an excellent time for letting others know about your various skills. You may be very successful in applying for any new position or job which requires you to learn and master new skills. You can do it. Make a mental image of what you need to achieve and direct your creative will towards this image daily. Anything you take on under The Magician card's powerful influence will strengthen your personality and belief in yourself. Begin to take risks and become more adaptable and versatile. People can't fail to notice you, as your powers are extraordinary. All this is fun too: you are learning to play it clever, not hard.

Reversed Meaning

The Magician reversed suggests there is a tricky or deceptive energy around you in the area of your question. You could even find an inability to be honest with yourself about something important. Perhaps you feel confused or overwhelmed by other people's thoughts or opinions rather than sticking to your own ideas. Someone around you could be tricky or slippery in business or in love. Remember, the issue will be power, not wisdom, in such a person. You could miss a very good opportunity by not believing in yourself when The Magician appears reversed, so do not lose your nerve, your faith, or give away your power to someone playing games. Try to stay honest with yourself and alert to others. All is not lost. The Magician will always help you if you are true to yourself.

II.

The High Priestess

RULING PLANET: MOON

DESCRIPTION

A mysterious, pensive goddess sits between two pillars beyond which is a vibrant garden filled with fruits of the pomegranate, a symbol of feminine power. The High Priestess is dressed in an undergarment of shimmering silver-white, her headdress contains the full moon and at her feet lies a crescent moon, reminders of her links to the power of the changing moon. Inward and serene, she does not reveal all her secrets, as suggested by the book of knowledge and wisdom in her lap and the half-revealed world through the pillars. She represents the mysterious goddess, the Divine Mother, the eternal feminine, and guards the gateway to the unknown. This unknown is the place of the Divine Mind, the Universal Mind, the great sea of being from which we all come, and to which we will return.

II. The High Priestess

Upright Meaning

The High Priestess appears when you need to link to your inner knowing and intuition. Something is not quite revealed at present and the only way to understand your options is to seek wisdom which will give you strength and hope. Sometimes you may feel changeable, like  the moon, with feelings fluctuating from hot to cold. Yet somewhere within this sense of uncertainty is a core of experience that will help you to move into the next phase. Ask yourself: "What do I really know of this person or situation?" While you wait and reflect on your gut-feeling response, you are like the High Priestess who sits and waits before allowing you access to the knowledge you seek. Remember, the High Priestess offers to connect you to the Divine Mind through her guardianship of the gateway.

Others may find you cool or unresponsive as you ponder on things before acting. You are in a pensive mood when you approach the temple of the High Priestess and you need peace and quiet to sort out your thoughts and feelings. When The High Priestess appears, you need to learn patience in all matters to do with the question asked. Things slow down and go through a natural cycle of withdrawal as you retreat into the mental sphere. Revelations will come to you from within, through dreams and daydreams, or maybe from talking to a wise or inspired woman who will be very helpful. Cultivate cool-headedness and reflection and don't give too much away. You know your heart still beats warmly about certain people and situations, but you need to be somewhat secretive for a short while. The moon's cycle is one month and it may take that long for matters to be revealed more fully. You stand in the hall of wisdom. Listen for the soundless voice within, which knows.

II. The High Priestess

Reversed Meaning

When you draw The High Priestess reversed, you will experience emotional highs and lows. You cannot seem to find the serenity of the High Priestess, or your wisdom and experience does not extend to your present situation. This is a cycle of learning to stay calm in circumstances fraught with difficulties. You may feel misunderstood or that you don't even understand yourself. It is very easy to act in haste at the moment, which you may regret later. Remind yourself that you are strong, and have already survived many troubles. Being at the gateway to the Universal Mind you have a choice of how to behave. The High Priestess, whether upright or reversed, wants you to stay calm and well grounded and to listen to sound, practical advice. If you remember your True Self, you can still find peace within. If you forget and become overwhelmed, you will feel only trouble and strife. One positive outcome of drawing The High Priestess reversed, is that you will feel more sensual and alive than you have for a while.

III.

The Empress

RULING PLANET: VENUS

DESCRIPTION

A richly dressed pregnant woman sits in a field of ripe grain that is abounding with life. On her head is a tiara of 12 sparkling stars, a symbol of the signs of the zodiac and the presence of universal forces manifest in our life on earth. Prosperous and calm, The Empress is mother nature in all her forms. As number three of the Major Arcana, she represents birth from the union of the two cards before her as well as growth, pregnancy, and fertility in all ventures. Her gown is decorated with acorns, the seeds of the oak tree, symbols of the wisdom of nature. This wisdom protects and nurtures the young, and also, when the time is right, casts out youthful energy to fend for itself. The acorns represent the idea of the potential power of the seed which is inherent in The Empress card.

III. The Empress

Upright Meaning

When you draw this card, you are entering a time of abundant creativity. You will experience a period of growth and harmony in your work and relationships. The Empress embodies the fertility of nature, so that whatever you are thinking of when selecting this card will flourish. Projects that you have been working on for some time now start to grow and bear fruit and provide a firm foundation for the future. Business partnerships and financial matters flourish under the abundant energy of the Empress. If you are in business, this card suggests that you expand your interests. At work open up your options, you will be noticed and appreciated. She is ever-pregnant, the mother of all, the lover of all, the Great Mother Goddess in her creative guise. You will feel a joy in life and a faith in the cycles which move the universe.

The Empress represents all that is desirable to the senses. Roses smell sweeter, touch is more loving, as all your senses are heightened. She is the Great Mother Goddess in her ecstatic union with her Beloved and so all relationships open out into a richer and more loving expression. The Empress blesses all unions, so drawing this card is an excellent omen for love and lovers, marriage, and children. You will feel more beautiful than you have for a while. Others are drawn to you for you appear somehow different. Magnetic and appealing, whether in business or in personal matters, you attract what is necessary for your growth. Everything receives an extra dash of chemistry and it is good to be alive. Wear rich colors, select perfumes to match your mood. Be romantic, spend time in nature, and relax in comfortable surroundings.

III. The Empress

Reversed Meaning

The challenge when receiving The Empress reversed is to keep believing in growth and opportunity, even when your way seems blocked. It may be that something or someone you believed would grow into significance in your life seems to have withdrawn. Upheavals can occur in relationships or housing and much of your old sense of security is under threat. The Empress reminds us of nature and there is a fallow period in every cycle where it appears nothing is happening. In reality, this is a very fertile time under the surface. If you fight this experience, you could find yourself feeling exhausted and angry. Hold onto your faith in the great cycles underlying all nature. Believe in your own creativity, in right action and right timing. Connection to the Empress requires that you practice love. She is the Divine Mother whose primary concern is love. She does not judge, but sees you in all your glory as one of the sparking jewels in the crown of her creation.

IV.

The Emperor

RULING SIGN: ARIES

DESCRIPTION

The Emperor sits on a solid cubic throne. He is a strong, mature man, giving the impression of worldly power and leadership. The Emperor represents the power of the masculine forces: dynamic ambition and a love of order and structure. His feet and legs are clad in armor, reminding us of his warrior past. His crown is heavy and encrusted with jewels, the sign of his worldly authority and responsibility. The background shows mountains and rocks, conveying a solidity and grounding. From his vantage point, the Emperor keeps an eye on everything in his domain. His powerful eye also represents our ability to look at ourselves from a new perspective and the courage to act upon those findings.

IV. The Emperor

Upright Meaning

Drawing The Emperor gives strength, vision, and purpose to your question. You have the willpower to achieve much in the near future, and you can fight for what you want if necessary. Now is the time to take control of the matter in question and be very clear about what you need to do. The Emperor gives you the ability to look honestly and practically at yourself. A masculine power is being activated by you either externally or internally. Mature and energetic, it links you to worldly wealth and power and is helpful as long as you are creative and active in your efforts. Doors open for you personally or professionally as this is a card of influence. The Emperor understands the way the world works. He may attract a strong partner to you, if you are seeking love. A time of sitting back or waiting is over and action is essential.

Open the doors to your own creativity and be bold about your decisions. Within you, masculine qualities are wanting expression. The appearance of The Emperor card suggests that you have influence at this time and may be in a position to help others. Start to order your concerns and matters will fall quickly into place. This is a time when you must stand up for your beliefs and what life experience has taught you. Stay alert and aware of all that is happening to you. You need to be in command of your life. You are now in a position to build upon the past and into the future because you will be given the gift of vision from the far-seeing Emperor. You begin to realize your place in the scheme of things and to be awake to the reasons why you are here at this particular time. Opportunities for personal and professional advancement abound in the future, so concentrate and build. The Emperor can bring dreams into reality.

Reversed Meaning

The Emperor reversed describes a time when you may feel all your resolve turn to water. You want to be strong, but you give up. Your willpower deserts you and for a while you feel weak and helpless. Equally, you may be attracted to people who turn out to be selfish and weak. One of the laws of life is that you rule or are ruled. Who is the ruler, within or outside of yourself, that holds power over you at the moment? The Emperor wants you to learn about your own power structures and make definite changes. Perhaps you do not get that job you applied for, or the adventure you planned falls through. All the more reason to ask yourself what really matters to you. Start to believe in your own values rather than those in authority over you. Be your own authority! This is a time of trial that may frustrate, annoy, or anger you enough to make some fundamental changes or re-evaluations in your life.

V.

The Hierophant

RULING SIGN: TAURUS

DESCRIPTION

The Hierophant is seen robed and crowned, serenely and kindly blessing the two priests who kneel before him. He holds a golden staff which terminates in the triple cross, symbolic of the levels of his wisdom. In the foreground lie two ornate, golden keys on a richly woven rug representing knowledge and wisdom as the key to religious and social order. As the teacher and spiritual master, the Hierophant upholds the social and religious order and encourages traditional ways and means of dealing with problems. His life of contemplation at a deep level gives him the capacity for new and fresh insights into age-old spiritual, social, or personal dilemmas.

V. The Hierophant

Upright Meaning

When dealing with current problems, The Hierophant advises it is best to take a methodical approach. At the moment, you need to create some order or routine in your life, for whatever the problem, it is best to adhere to tried and true ways. As you feel more secure, a sense of mental correctness will begin to assert itself, and you will know what to do. The Hierophant loves the comforting rhythm of routine and if you can create this you will feel more peaceful about the question in your mind. The Hierophant offers guidance in his connection between the outermost and the innermost places. If truly and diligently seeking answers, a new insight or fresh way of seeing present concerns will pop into your mind.

Your values come into question when The Heirophant is drawn, so ask yourself what is really important to you and where you are prepared to give and take. Ask an old friend or teacher for advice, as you are willing to learn and be guided at this time. Listen also to your own "still small voice" reminding you of all your gifts and resources. In order to connect to the right choice, you must quiet your noisy, "monkey" mind and its ceaseless chatter. The Hierophant wants to raise his hand and bless you with kindliness and concern, so be at peace over present worries. Regarding your question, you need to make some form of commitment at the moment. In love, you need to move to a more formalized relationship or marriage. In business, it is good to make binding contracts that are comfortable for all concerned. For health, you need to commit to proper care of your body; not just exercise but proper rest.

V. The Hierophant

Reversed Meaning

When reversed, The Hierophant brings disorder. Someone you meet may cause you to question long-held values. Perhaps you feel resentful, having been the "good girl" or "good boy" for too long. You may want to fly in the face of convention and do something totally outrageous. Where you have felt long-term commitments, you may want to break out or rebel. Marriages, friendships, and old patterns will go through a period of upheaval at this time. You may wish to form a new marriage or union or feel attracted to someone who has a very different background or culture from you. The Hierophant reversed wants you to re-examine your traditionally held beliefs and old routines as it is time to change some habitual ways of thinking and behaving. The Hierophant is a spiritual card and so blesses this time of questioning and upheaval as a necessary part of your growth. You will emerge with more of a sense of who you are and what is your true path.

VI.

The Lovers

RULING SIGN: GEMINI

DESCRIPTION

The sun shines brightly behind the figure of an angel pouring down benevolent, heavenly influences. In the foreground are the two naked figures of Adam and Eve. The image embodies the ancient idea of opposites which, like *Yin* and *Yang,* complement each other and cannot exist alone. That humans are made for relationship is a key idea in this card. We also have an instinct to work in harmony with the universe, as shown by the woman who, seeking the unseen world, gazes into the cloud. The snake is a sacred symbol of earth-knowing. Listening with its very body to the vibrations that abound, it whispers into Eve's ear imparting old earth wisdom. The man observes the woman and may be guided by her intuition at this time. The design suggests a reliance on instincts and feelings when making certain important choices.

VI. The Lovers

Upright Meaning

When The Lovers card appears you are often, although not always, facing an important choice about a relationship. Your intuition tells you that what is happening is very important, even crucial. Indeed, present conditions are here to teach you about choices of the heart. Even if your question relates to business or some other matter, you will find you are making decisions more from the heart than the head. This card suggests more than one option is presenting itself. Allow intuition to be your guide in making decisions for the moment. Something will begin to feel right and you must act on that feeling. Listen to the wisdom of the snake that whispers its message to you, just as it is whispering to Eve in the card. The snake is always true to its own path, it never deviates to please anyone. The snake knows the way, just as something within you senses your correct direction or path. You feel instinctively when your foot is upon that path and there is overwhelming joy in this knowledge. If, however, you walk the path you think you *should* take or the one your head tells you is right, you will feel unhappy in the core of your being.

The Lovers card also speaks about love and lovers. Stories and myths tell of the importance of a "sacred marriage" to spiritual growth. This inner union with the Beloved of the Soul is as important as outer union with an earthly beloved. You may have dreams of uniting with another, or a sense of things coming together. When The Lovers card is realized within you through a spiritual union, you will experience grace. The card augurs well for love and lovers and opens the heart to the possibility of love in its many forms. Romance, the possibility of a new relationship, or the reawakening of an old flame is on the horizon. You will feel strong emotions, a stirring for life and love. Attractions and passions run strong at the moment. Remember, these attractions may not be fleeting, they hold the possibility of leading to a real and lasting union.

Reversed Meaning

When you draw The Lovers reversed you are facing a period of difficulty around a choice you have to make, or a choice made in the past that has returned in another form. You may find one of your relationships is based on rocky foundations. One person may love more than the other, or there may be deception around you at work or play. Because The Lovers card wants you to learn to make deep choices of the heart based on your own inner knowing rather than entirely rational deductions, you may feel your concerns swinging from the heart to the head continually. You must ask yourself honestly: "What do I really feel or want?" The Lovers archetype will begin to help you once you are willing to deeply explore your feelings. It also asks you to be wise and wait for the right time to make the hard choices, be they in business or personal matters. Follow the instinctual knowing of the snake, who knows the importance of your right path. You may have stepped upon the path chosen by reason, or the one you thought would bring joy, but found it feels empty. Trust your heart again and you will feel the return of the surge of life.

VII.

The Chariot

DESCRIPTION

The charioteer stands upright in a vehicle drawn by two magical horses, one black, one white, representing the opposing forces in human nature. There are no reins. The horses are commanded by the sheer will of the charioteer, the invisible reins of the mind. *The Upanishads*, ancient, sacred Indian texts, speak of the importance of the horses of desire being held in check by the inner charioteer. The canopy is covered with stars symbolizing our cosmic origins. On the shoulders of the charioteer are two half-moons, which link him to the power of the moon and indicate his mastery over fluctuations of emotional energy. The chariot moves away from a walled city which is now quite distant.

VII. The Chariot

Upright Meaning

The appearance of The Chariot suggests you are in a period of movement and change. You may have been struggling for some time with choices that had to be made and now feel the freedom and power of your own will as you surge forward over obstacles. It is time to become the driver of your life "vehicle." Shut out the foolishness of greed and grasping which goes on all about you in the world. You have learned a lot in the past few months and this experience will be useful as you face the next phase with strength and mastery. You now know that nothing is black or white, but rather a blend of energies, like the horses pulling the chariot. The Chariot speaks of mastery, balance, and understanding of the dual energies of the feminine (Number 3, The Empress) and the masculine (Number 4, The Emperor). The Chariot teaches you to be in respectful control of these dual forces as well as your animal instincts, so they may serve you well.

The Chariot denotes success in the question you have asked and implies that you must take a strong stand in present concerns. Your mind needs to be strong yet flexible, like the hand of an artist with utmost control of the brushstroke. Triumph comes from experience and persistence, it will not be merely handed to you. You have earned this time of leaping forward. You are moving away from the "old city" like the charioteer in the card. This old city may be the old thoughts and beliefs where you learned the lessons of choice; or it may refer to people, jobs, houses. Now at the end of one part of the journey which has been a struggle, The Chariot takes you into a new adventure based on a better understanding of yourself through experience. Be bold and confident, without arrogance. Act with all your concentration regarding your question and victory will be yours.

Reversed Meaning

The Chariot reversed indicates a disruptive influence. Travel or other plans may become confused or be abandoned. Perhaps your self-confidence lessens as you try to sort out the many conflicting issues around the question. You may find your will disappearing in negative thoughts, or you may seek to flee from harsh reality using your usual form of escape. Someone may be trying to dominate you or forcing you into doing something. Or you may be the one who is trying to control things. The Chariot wants you to stop and look carefully at what is happening. Progress can still be made if you can make sense of things and do not resort to force or fall into confusion. You need to learn the wisdom of the True Self before the wheel of progress can turn fully. Watch out for the negative inner voice which tries to dominate you or rides roughshod over your instincts and feelings. Steady yourself as if you were an unsettled animal by calm, repetitive words and thoughts. If you look at the image in the reversed card you will notice that the animals are uppermost and the charioteer is now dominated by them. The Tarot teaches that the animal nature needs to be respected, but held in check by the will.

VIII.

Strength

RULING SIGN: LEO

DESCRIPTION

A goddess in a white robe closes the mouth of a large lion. The goddess shows no fear, she looks down at the lion with gentleness and love, closing its mouth with her hands. The goddess is a symbol of human consciousness and the lion represents our instinctual or animal nature. On looking at this card, one is struck by the relationship between the goddess and the lion. Their dynamic reminds us of our relationship to our own animal nature which, according to the Tarot, needs loving attention to be strong, playful, and tuned to our instincts. The figure eight symbol of infinity appears above the head of the goddess in the card, representing the eternal dance between these two sides of our nature. In ancient archaeological temples, figurines, myths, and stories, the Great Mother Goddess is seen with tame lions. She rode them, transformed herself into them, drove a chariot drawn by lions, and lions protected her temple gates.

VIII. Strength

Upright Meaning

The Strength card offers love as the way to approach any problem that confronts you. The Tarot sees strength as a quality of gentleness and self-knowledge rather than force, which is almost contradictory to modern attitudes. You need to be strong at the moment, and you will be given the fortitude to act. Love alone can conquer fear and anger. In the strength of loving you can find your true power. Unity is another form of power. You need to be united within yourself and in the area in question. Think about the question you have in your mind and look at the card. Is your approach harmonious and playful in relationship to this question or area of your life? When you feel this unity and love at work, you can also experience the wonder inscribed in the infinity sign above the head of the goddess.

Another way of approaching your question is to feel the inner power of the lion, the king of the beasts. His pride and vitality can be yours at the moment. The goddess in the image shows us how to treat the wild animal

of our own body and nature. A badly treated animal reacts with anger; the animal treated lovingly will respond with love. Love yourself and you can really love others. Meditating on the Strength image can help link you to an eternal, spiritual strength which will begin to radiate out from you. Even if you are feeling unwell or low in energy, drawing the Strength card augurs well for a recovery of health and emotional well-being. You cannot fail to be noticed when the Strength card appears,

VIII. Strength

for this quality of love, strong convictions, and peace will draw others to you like moths to a flame. Your confidence will improve, as will your relationships with people who may have been difficult lately. You can reconcile old battles within yourself at this time, as your sense of self is strengthened. Stand up for yourself and people will listen and appreciate you.

Reversed Meaning

When the Strength card appears reversed you may experience a loss of vitality or an illness. You could feel separated from love and unable to perceive the mysterious connections which make life wonderful. Perhaps you are not listening to your inner animal self which has been trying to tell you not to associate with certain people, or that you need more rest or exercise. When this integral relationship between conscious self and animal nature is unbalanced, you can feel unworthy and miserable. Imagine a sick, caged lion with a dull coat that has no way of reaching its beloved plains. This animal is in you. You must free it, allow it to regain its noble bearing, which is, of course, your own nobility. You will soon need your courage more than ever, so rest and recuperate. Shortly your physical, emotional, and moral strength will return.

IX.

The Hermit

RULING SIGN: VIRGO

DESCRIPTION

The Hermit appears in the figure of a heavily hooded, grey-cloaked old man, The Ancient of Days. He holds a long staff in his left hand and in his right hand blazes a lantern containing a shining, golden star. This is the archetypal Wise Old Man/Woman whose wisdom shines from within, although the outward appearance is humble. In the darkness, this wise old guide is there to serve us by shining the light on the unknown path. Ever patient, the Hermit gives the impression of one who has survived the difficulties of life in a strong, solitary way. The mountains where the Hermit lives represent a place of spiritual growth and achievement that has nothing to do with worldly success. The Hermit is the wise counsellor, the healer, and the guide.

IX. The Hermit

Upright Meaning

The Hermit portends a period of retreat and contemplation. You have been through a period of energetic activity and now it is time to stop, reflect, and plan. Whatever the question, the answer will not come through external activity and striving. The Hermit is the Wise One who represents our Inner Self, which is always trying to illuminate the truth for us. The card depicts a hermit holding his lantern up to show the way, and reassures that light will be shone on your uncertainty at the moment. The enlightenment of a new way will be given, even if you thought you had tried all avenues. Something is not understood and answers need to be sought in the stillness of the heart. "Where is my way? Who am I really? What is my true path through this? How may I find peace?" These are some of the questions to contemplate.

Whatever your question regards, a wise friend or counsellor may be sought at this time. Do not expect quick or easy answers, for the Hermit's way is slow and cautious. In fact, there is a warning against rushing into anything when you select The Hermit. If you can listen to a counsellor, or tune in to your own inner guide, you will find a sense of meaning beginning to formulate. Something will unravel and you will see the thread that has led you to this point. Wrap the great cloak of the Hermit around you. This mystical cloak is the symbol of the way the Wise One is shrouded, even in a crowd. Within the cloak you can find the mystery of silence and stillness. Be silent and calm. Every effort you make towards inner guidance at this time will be answered.

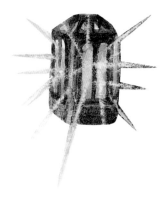

IX. The Hermit

Reversed Meaning

The Hermit reversed warns you to be cautious; you may be ignoring important messages from your body, your inner voice, or concerned friends or counsellors. You need to take time out but you may be trying to keep up the old level of activity and not listening to some deep prompting to take a break. Perhaps it is someone around you behaving this way and you find yourself in the frustrating role of helpless bystander while they continue on destructively. Whatever is happening, you may feel angry and reject offers of help. You may even reject the wisdom of your own dreams and intuitions, or this book. Remember, the great souls were tempted when very close to achieving a goal. No matter how bad things seem you are probably on the brink of an important change. Don't give up in despair or anger. Do take some time out to be alone and think about what can realistically be done to create a change, however small.

X.

The Wheel of Fortune

RULING PLANET: JUPITER

DESCRIPTION

The Wheel of Fortune describes the cyclic nature of existence. The universe was born in a whirling motion as galaxies gave birth to galaxies and spiraled forth myriads of stars. Atoms and molecules spin us into existence. We are born, we live, we die. We return to the other realm, and maybe we are born again, and so on. The Wheel of Fortune is depicted on the card as a turning wheel. It is a mandala, the symbol of wholeness. A magical, golden-winged being appears in each of the four corners of the card: an angel, an eagle, a cow, and a lion respectively. These beings represent the fixed signs of the zodiac, the principles that do not change in the ever-turning cycles of life. Everything that happens in the universe takes place within a fixed frame of reference. One complete turning of the wheel represents the year with its ever-repeating four seasons.

X. The Wheel of Fortune

Upright Meaning

The Wheel indicates that you have ended one major cycle of learning and are ready to enter a new stage of life. You reap now what you have sown in the past. Much has been learned by waiting and watching and now is the time to act. Lucky opportunities may fall into your lap and you are ready for change. Trust the cycles of your life and the wisdom of your own rhythm. Don't worry about decisions, trust your instincts and step into the new. Be open and trusting in the possibilities of life. When you close one door another opens, and at present you are standing before a new door. There is no need to look back, you have all you need with you. Events beyond your control may astound you as your destiny is triggered by the powerful turning of The Wheel.

There is a fundamental order which underlies your life and that of the universe. You are a child of the universe as much as every flower, tree, rock, and stream. Having stepped into another level of yourself, it is important to recognize how far you have come. What goes around comes around. What goes up must come down. These commonplace sayings draw their truth from realizing the position of The Wheel beneath our lives, always turning, never still, even when we feel nothing is happening. In the rest of the journey you will need to learn the great lesson of The Wheel: inner peace. The middle, or hub, of The Wheel is the mystical quiet place. The spokes of The Wheel turn, but that place in the middle is untouched by the turning. This is the mystery; the place of peace and calm, stillness within motion.

X. The Wheel of Fortune

Reversed Meaning

When you select The Wheel reversed, you may experience a sense of going backwards. It is as if you have boarded the wrong train and can do nothing until it arrives at its destination. You may feel that you have had bad luck, fortune has been unkind, or matters are beyond your control. These are symptoms of The Wheel reversed. Indeed, this is not your most fortunate time but as cycles bring change, there will be a return to good in your life. How should you live through such a period of hindrances? The Wheel wants you to contemplate the circular nature of fate: nations and their leaders rise and fall; one fashion replaces another. Only the deep inner values are eternal. Remember, our greatest wealth is knowing we are complete in ourselves. You need nothing more, lack nothing. Decide how you can live today with a sense of fun and grace even when there are delays and frustration. The discipline of smiling in the face of adversity will probably turn The Wheel once again to good fortune.

XI.

Justice

RULING SIGN: LIBRA

DESCRIPTION

A richly dressed goddess sits between two pillars. In her left hand she holds the scales of justice and in her right a sword is held upright. This sword is a symbol of the power of truth, wisdom, and order. The figure represents the serious nature of appraisal and judgement that is justice. In Egyptian mythology, it was said that after death, the heart–soul was weighed on the scales of the goddess Maat, against her symbol, the Feather of Truth. Justice in the Tarot represents logical, clear-minded, and unbiased decisions. She reminds us of another justice which is mystical and connected to the soul, represented by the golden light behind the veil. Justice exists at the middle of the numerical sequence of the Tarot, so she holds the central position, one of balance.

XI. Justice

Upright Meaning

When you draw the Justice card your ability to logically and calmly look at your present problem is excellent. Because you can negotiate well at the moment, and can put aside strong emotions, you can see the larger picture clearly. You can work towards easing old conflicts, as agreement is now possible. Connected to the powerful All Seeing Eye of the goddess Maat, you can now see clearly and  dispassionately. You can sense falsehood or illusion, as you have your own Feather of Truth just now. Weigh things up and see who or what is left wanting and who respects you. Feelings are best put to one side and cool, rational action will achieve the best results. You need to act with honesty and face matters fairly. People who have led you a merry dance for some time need to be confronted, maybe left behind or urged towards a more lasting commitment. In everything, stand back and let your inner voice judge the situation and do not allow yourself to be swayed by emotion or manipulation.

   Imagine you hold a sword forged in the fire of truth. This sword will help you to make any decisions you face. Perhaps, like the boy-king Arthur, you have had to pull the sword unstuck from a rock or difficult place in your life. It will now be your ally, and others will sense you are well armed and worthy of respect. Make lists and work through them systematically. Eliminate what is non-essential with your sword of discrimination. You may need to let go of old parts of your life that are no longer useful or life-giving. Sometimes the Justice card will speak of a marriage or a lasting business venture. Justice may need to make ties legal and binding; or to break ties that no longer serve the people involved. Justice also connects you to a deeper truth about your life and your

destiny. A deeper law is being revealed to you. Ideas and images will surface, showing you who you are and how things are being made fair in their own way in your life.

Reversed Meaning

"It's not fair!" may be the cry on your lips when you receive the Justice card reversed. Indeed, you may be encountering injustice, either in a legal sense or in life. There are laws underpinning the universe which are not understood by our modern, rational, scientific minds. It may be that you are swimming against the tide, trying to be something or someone you are not. The Justice card reversed will throw you up time and time again on the shore if you battle against your True Self. Suddenly, when the light begins to penetrate your mind, you see clearly what you must do in order to restore harmony and peace. In truth, you need to eliminate excess and you will have no lack. On an outer level you may have to deal with the mundane workings of the law, or cope with unfair treatment from someone. It is the way you respond to such trials that will bring out the power of Justice to tip the scales your way again.

XII.

The Hanged Man

RULING PLANET: NEPTUNE

DESCRIPTION

In this mystical image a man is suspended by the right foot from a tree in the shape of a cross. The man is hanging upside down, but is not nailed as a Christ figure. Is he suffering or not? The mood of this card is strange for the man does not seem to be in agony, his head is surrounded with rays of light and his face is deeply entranced. The rays of light represent the enlightenment that comes from suffering. The growing tree on which he hangs is called the World Tree, as its roots are deep in the underworld and its branches reach to heaven. In the Norse myth, Odin, god of the hanged, learned many mysteries from the runes, poetry, and magic as he sacrificed himself by hanging on a tree for nine days and nights.

XII. The Hanged Man

Upright Meaning

The Hanged Man brings a period of sacrifice into your life. You may have to give up something you once thought was essential for your happiness. Like the enlightened man in the image, however, you will not suffer agony from this sacrifice. You need to look at things from a different angle when you select this card, and you will be given a fresh point of view. Like the figure in the card, you are in a cycle of intense inner growth. Nothing much may seem to be happening on the outside, but you will be filled with a sense of wonder about your life that will be hard to explain to others. Worldly matters seem to be upside down. Let things go into suspension for a short while. It is imperative that you find the peace in stillness. You will know you have found this peace when you have let go sufficiently, for you will be calm and unconcerned about usual worries. Like a plant that does not appear to be growing, you are putting down roots beneath the surface.

Suspended between two realities, you hang between the waking world and the deeper world of spirit, fairytale, and myth. Or you may be left hanging in a decision you need to make. Many different parts of your life will begin to fit together like pieces of a jigsaw, and you will make new connections. Powerful dreams whose images remain with you throughout the day could be your greatest guide at the moment. This is a time of healing for you. Music, painting, being in nature, especially by the sea, will all help in the healing process. This is a turning point in your life. Like a butterfly in a cocoon, surrender to life as it transforms you. You do not need to strive. You will emerge from this time more adaptable, more flexible in your thinking and able to see a way ahead that is more true to you than you had dreamed possible.

XII. The Hanged Man

Reversed Meaning

The Hanged Man reversed signals the end of a cycle of suffering, sacrifice, or indecision. Do not make any unnecessary sacrifices now. Start to attend to matters that have been left hanging or pending for some time. The Hanged Man warns you to act with caution and reflection but be wary of making decisions that are too materialistic or concrete. Recently you may have felt the need to withdraw and look within. Question some of your old values, beliefs and attitudes as well as the way your life is going in the outer world. Reflect on all your experiences and this will bring change. It is good for you spiritually to question externals, not to take things at face value. Whenever you begin to listen to your inner knowing and your instincts, your outer life must change. Know that you are moving from suffering to joy. The butterfly of The Self emerges from its cocoon and spreads its glistening wings. The great wisdom of the *Cabala* teaches that the reason for existence is delight, not misery.

XIII.

Death

RULING SIGN: SCORPIO

DESCRIPTION

A skeleton dressed in black armor rides a beautiful white horse. He carries a black banner depicting an ornate white Mystic Rose which signifies life. People stand or kneel before the skeleton as he approaches as does the inevitable, painful truth that death comes to us all. Far in the background blazes a rising sun, the emblem of rebirth and the soul's eternal life. Life depends on constant transformation from moment to moment. Death, as part of life, is integral to the Tarot's teaching and reminds us of our mortality but adds the promise of life eternal.

XIII. Death

Upright Meaning

The Death card in the Tarot marks a very positive change. Old situations in your life which have outlived their usefulness fall away and you can begin anew. Destruction is a natural part of the cycle of life. Our bodies daily kill old cells and are rejuvenated with new cells. Just as leaves fall and make way for new growth, it is important for "dead wood" to be removed from your life in order for you to grow. Fears naturally arise at this time  of letting go of the old and you may cling to the known. This fear is the protector of the old and our friend. Yet, psychologically, part of you must fade out for the new growth to occur. Maybe you need to leave behind some old beliefs or attitudes that once held true; or externally, maybe it is a job, a house, a person or any other part of your life which must now make way for the new.

The Death card signals a joyful transformation even though you may experience fear and uncertainty. There will be a period of transition but you can expect a brand-new outlook and fresh hopes. Relationships move to a new level or, inevitably, some may end. Those relationships which survive this major change will be re-enlivened. You will experience a sense of real emotional growth as you begin to understand that you have been recently living through a kind of initiation which you have had to endure alone. Death promises light at the end of the tunnel and the birth of a new era in your life, just as the sun's rays radiate beyond the skeleton in the card. Let go and there will be rebirth for you just around the corner.

XIII. Death

Reversed Meaning

When you draw the Death card reversed, you may be experiencing an impasse or deadlock in some area of your life. Perhaps you are holding on to something which is actually an obstacle hindering your movement forward. This stagnation is usually born of fear of the unknown. It is, however, causing a blockage in your life which cannot be maintained. Eventually, like it or not, something will have to give way as life wants you to move on. You may also be holding on to, or suppressing, your feelings of grief or anger. Let these feelings go and you will be surprised how quickly things can change. You are on the verge of a new beginning, only fear now holds you back. Let love into your heart in whatever way you can, for it is love which casts out fear and doubt. Love will always find the way.

XIV.

Temperance

RULING SIGN: SAGITTARIUS

DESCRIPTION

A great white angel with beautiful red wings stands with one foot on the ground and the other in the water. In her hands she holds two golden chalices between which she seems to be pouring water. This interchange of liquid depicts the dynamic of constant change. Her eyes are downcast and her face is concentrated but serene. Beside her stands a clump of tall green leaves and yellow irises. Iris was the Greek goddess of the rainbow, so these flowers symbolise hope after the storms of life. A small road rises from the pool and leads into the distant hills, ending brilliantly in a shining sun. This represents the possible pathway of our lives when emerging from the correct balance. *Tempare*, a Latin word meaning to mix or combine, is the origin of the naming of the Temperance card. To find the right mixture of the four elements in one's life is to find harmony. Temperance is serenity and balance, the essence of harmony.

XIV. Temperance

Upright Meaning

Receiving the Temperance card shows you have passed through a difficult and fearful time and are now able to reap the benefits of facing your fears. You will have the sense of something filling a void in your life; something which imparts a sense of wonder. Temperance also brings the gift of perfect timing to your actions. There is a blending of perfect ingredients; perhaps the best person is found for the job; a soul mate becomes a partner, and so on. An archangel or goddess is traditionally associated with the  Temperance card and brings to you the feeling of being close to the Source. This is a far cry from where you have been and it is only because you have passed through a dark time that you can appreciate the promise of the irises in the card. The irises, a symbol of the rainbow, suggests the wonder and hope of a fresh earth after the rain. This rain, for you, may have been a time of tears or of overwhelming feelings, or it could have been a cleansing, making way for the new.

This time of coming through darkness is to teach you to value your feelings and to take care of the precious liquid of your soul. Just as the angel pours this precious liquid from chalice to chalice, you need to consider carefully where to give the essence of yourself. All too often we can give away that which is essential for our well-being by overworking, or spreading our lives too thinly, leaving no time for ourselves and our loved ones. When you receive this card you can no longer burn the candle at both ends, for if you do it warns that your physical or emotional health will suffer. The lessons of Temperance are firstly that you need to allow time for recovery and creativity; secondly, to learn the right mix for yourself to create moderation in all things.

XIV. Temperance

Reversed Meaning

Temperance reversed indicates you are in an excessively busy or unbalanced time. You may feel the pressures and stresses of the modern world pushing down on you. Because you are so stressed you could easily make a mistake regarding your question. You could fail to take into account all the factors involved and be unable to make the compromises necessary for a desirable outcome. Make time to consider your question in a balanced way, or you could regret not doing so later. You may also find you are being tested regarding your values or philosophy. Again, do not overreact. You need such tests to consolidate your position. See this difficult time as an opportunity to stand firm in your basic beliefs. Temperance here speaks of you being tempered in the fire of life, as if you were a sword in the making. A sword is taken from the burning fire only to be plunged in icy water many times to make it supple and strong. Know that you will be strengthened in the present circumstances to continue on your spiritual journey.

XV.

The Devil

RULING SIGN: CAPRICORN

DESCRIPTION

The laughing devil image dominates this card. He sits perched on a stone to which are chained the naked figures of a man and woman. Like an over-powering force, he seems to bind the two figures in some strange way. The Devil appears as half animal, half man, showing his lusty, animal nature. The man and woman also have animal features, claws and tails, indicating the possibility of becoming entrapped by one's lower desires. The chains bind-ing them around the neck are loose and could easily be pulled over their heads. In ancient tales, Pan, the god on whom this image is designed, was called the life-giver. He is a force to be reckoned with, the power of our own nature and desires. The lesson is not to become bound by our desires but to know and respect them. The Devil should be approached with a sense of fun. Our own failings and foibles are often very funny.

XV. The Devil

Upright Meaning

The Devil foretells a time when, like in the image, you can find yourself tied to fearful or obsessive conduct. You may be bound to the fear of losing money, a person, or some role that you feel you cannot do without. When you recognize this feeling of bondage, do all in your power to seek liberation! Recognize that mostly this world's problems are caused by illusion. We hold various illusions that money, other worldly goods, or power will bring us happiness. Happiness of course comes from within, from knowing oneself and walking our own path in freedom. The Devil holds up the temptation of something illusionary, and at the moment you are quite vulnerable to control or manipulation. Or you may be the manipulator. Longing for something that will temporarily satisfy your material desires could obsess you. In these ways, you are further bound. When you draw The Devil card, you can easily make a wrong choice regarding your question. You need to examine the realities and practicalities of anything you are considering and make decisions not based on fear, desire, or guilt.

The Devil is a card which speaks of power. This is often expressed as the misuse of sexual or financial power in the modern world. When you draw The Devil, you may be susceptible to unhealthy attachments or to jealous obsessions about someone. Pan, the ancient god who inspired this image, was celebrated for his fertility and power of procreation. This is more the true energy of The Devil card. Whichever way the Devil is manifesting his lusty presence in your life, see it as an opportunity to face some of your old fears and obsessions. Jung spoke about coming into relationship with your "shadow" as a very important stage of growth. Everyone has dark and secret places which they would rather not acknowledge. Confronting these less pleasant parts of yourself is what the Devil requires before you feel the freedom and release of powerful, creative energy into your life.

Finally, the Devil wants us to bathe our souls with laughter. Be willing to laugh at yourself and see the ridiculous side of the Devil. The two figures in the image are not really bound and the Devil is enjoying it all immensely.

Reversed Meaning

Freedom is the keyword when you draw The Devil card reversed. You may have recently been through a very difficult or fearful period, but you will emerge from this time triumphant. You can no longer be restrained or kept in any position of powerlessness as you have learned the lessons concerning this particular clash with greed or misuse of power. You can walk away from bad situations with spirit and dignity. The Devil reversed marks the end of a period of a kind of enslavement, maybe to a person, to a job, or even to success. Your energy for life is uplifted. Everything has more zest and appeal. Having broken through the veil of illusion that says we need externals to make us happy, you can begin to experience inner freedom. You will be filled with laughter and a sense

of fun. This can manifest as absolute joy in life or it may be expressed sexually. Your sex life improves!

XVI.

The Tower

RULING PLANET: MARS

DESCRIPTION

The Tower is a wild, violent, and exciting card. A large tower has been struck by lightning. Where the lightning has struck, fires are beginning to burn. Stark and disturbing, we see the figures of a man and a woman flung head-first out of the tower, falling helplessly. What has happened to cause such sudden wild events? The card is a depiction of the sudden chaotic changes of life. Things can never be quite the same again. The earth moves, and the tower tumbles down. The tower is the old way of thinking we construct in our minds which tells us that we, like Rapunzel, are separate and different from the rest of life. The Tower seems to emerge from a high mountain peak which indicates the spiritual basis for the seeming revolutions in our lives.

XVI. The Tower

Upright Meaning

The Tower portends a dramatic change in your life. You may have felt something brewing, like the build-up to a storm, but the actual change when it happens will be swift. Sometimes The Tower's influence operates like the thunderbolt you see on the card, and you find you are abruptly thrown out of the old ways of constructing your life or thinking. Someone you meet may bring this thunderbolt, or it can come out of the blue in other ways. It also operates like an earthquake so that some of the less stable forms and structures of your mind's invention fall down. Old bondages are thrust aside as you experience a new sense of freedom. Wake up and become aware of inner truth is the message of The Tower card. You may lose your temper and say things you thought were properly buried. You need to clear the air. One of the shocks which The Tower foretells is the surfacing of the truth at last. The lid can no longer be kept on secrets, so be prepared for some truth-telling and truth-hearing.

These upheavals you are facing are necessary, and you will come to see the reasons when the dust settles. Sometimes The Tower indicates a health problem or breakdown of some part of the body or mind. More often it will be a change of an old routine or structure to which you are accustomed and do not question. Expect the unexpected. The best-laid plans collapse into chaos at this time. Remember the old joke: *You want to know how to make God laugh? Tell him your plans.* All you can do is weather the storm and pick up the pieces afterwards. Have faith that new plans will emerge which are more in line with your true direction. The Tower reminds you of your greatest gift to the world: to live your life expressing your uniqueness to the best of your ability. Until you, the individual, have changed, the world will not change. Remember, although The Tower card is dark the beautiful light of hope is already beginning to rain down.

XVI. The Tower

Reversed Meaning

A change you have been somewhat expecting is upon you. Perhaps it has already happened and you are starting to sort it out. The Tower either reversed or upright means change and upheaval, but reversed it is often more manageable. Maybe you have had a premonition of change but been unable to prepare for it. There could still be surprises in store in the coming few days, so don't rest easy yet. The Tower is really about how we humans construct rigid ways of living outside of any relationship with the rest of nature. It challenges our view of ourselves as separate and different from the rest of life. Perhaps it takes a disaster to unite people, so through dramatic events The Tower will bring you into contact with your True Self and others in new and exciting ways. Be flexible, truthful, and willing to be surprised by life and this will be a very productive phase.

XVII.

The Star

RULING SIGN: AQUARIUS

DESCRIPTION

A naked goddess kneels with one foot in a pool of swirling blue water and one knee on the grassy bank. She is pouring crystal-clear water from two jugs. One stream of water pours back into the pool and the other pours over the bank making little rivulets on the ground and watering the flowers which are beginning to bloom. The Star shows the goddess in her form of nourisher of the earth and ourselves. She is the Divine Mother of cosmic balance, and in her actions she demonstrates the balance of the four elements. Through the waters of our loving essence, we nurture ourselves and the earth. The clear blue sky (air) contains the cosmic fire as stars. The Star is the card which rules meditation as the way to balance within ourselves.

XVII. The Star

Upright Meaning

The Star indicates a time of new hope in life. You may have
experienced a change of plans but now matters can take
shape. More in tune with infinite wisdom than
you may realize, your life is beginning to show its new
direction. The Star in the design is a knowing,
loving star and is supported by seven little stars
representing help from friends and loved ones and
from your own life-experience.
Meditate on the ways of nature. "Consider
the lilies of the field," says the Bible. They
neither toil nor spin, they simply *are* in
a state of trust and acceptance, being their true selves.
It is through meditation that cosmic balance, which
nourishes all parts of ourselves, may be achieved. The
number seven is associated with learning by experience and
becoming humble and wise. So much has been achieved
already in the matter of your question. Look
around for helpers within and outside of yourself. You will
be pleasantly surprised by the assistance you receive.

You can now move forward and use your talents in
a positive way. Doors are beginning to open to you
and the world is unfolding new horizons. Having been noticed for your
abilities and for simply being yourself, you too can become a kind of star.
You will be acknowledged for things you have done which you may have
almost given up on in the past. Talents you did not recognize before may
emerge. Success is assured in the area of your question if you can have faith
and stay optimistic and calm. The Star offers a constant guiding light by

which we may navigate the sea of life. Trust the guidance of The Star and you will be led in the area of your question. For some people The Star indicates a linking to some kind of occult knowledge, particularly astrology.

Reversed Meaning

You may have lost faith in your question when you draw The Star reversed. Hopes appear dashed and you can be full of doubts. You may feel unwell or uninspired to look after yourself properly, or that your talents are meaningless and there is no way to be seen for who you really are. The Star is always there to guide your way, but it seems to have disappeared. However, The Star never really goes away, it is just that you cannot perceive it at present. It is operating in the dark or is hidden from view. You need to trust in the unseen more than usual, for you could otherwise become depressed or feel hopeless in the area of your query. There is, however, no point in bashing your head against a brick wall, so retreat and wait for the pinpoint of light to reappear in your sky. Meditate on the simple, daily cycles of nature. There has never been a day when the sun did not bring light into the darkness.

XVIII.

The Moon

RULING SIGN: PISCES

DESCRIPTION

This strange card depicts two dogs baying beneath a moon which is both full and crescent. Surreal images of a lobster emerging from the water and forbidding grey towers appear. Something in the card evokes fear, as we have all experienced the "long dark night of the soul." At night familiar things can look peculiar and different, even frightening. This card is like a dreamscape with its disturbing images that sometimes haunt our dreams and evoke fearful imaginings. The Moon is connected to the changeable unconscious world which we can only reach in dreams. In ancient times, the moon was seen as a symbol of the Great Mother Goddess. She exists as the triple goddess: the new moon or Maiden; the full moon as Mother; and the waning moon as Hecate, the crone or Wise One. The moon in all its phases is part of the wisdom symbolism in the Tarot and appears on many of the cards. Look especially at The High Priestess and The Chariot.

XVIII. The Moon

Upright Meaning

You are now in a period of heightened sensitivity and can be more creative and imaginative than usual. Your dreams may be vivid, for the Moon rules that time when we sleep, opening to the unconscious world. New ideas are formulated and explored during sleep. We are actually being remade. Sometimes when you select this card, you may feel overwhelmed as it can be a difficult time to set limits on yourself or others close to you. Dreams and dream images can persist throughout your day and you may find yourself absorbed in daydreams, sometimes disturbing and confusing ones. Actually, you are caught between the waking and sleeping worlds, a most creative place to be, so use the time for imaginative and creative projects. Moonlight also sets the place for romance and creates the atmosphere of love. Spend languid time with loved ones, or surround yourself with music, poetry, and literature that is close to your heart.

There are dangers when in the realm of the Moon. You can be misinterpreted by others who cannot understand things that seem so obvious to you by the light of the Moon. You can also misinterpret your own dreams and visions, so you need to keep one foot very grounded. Watch out for self-deception, as it is easy to muddle your thoughts or emotions at this time. The moon is renowned for its psychic energy, so your intuition will be powerful at the moment. However, it is quite difficult to receive psychic messages about yourself at this time. Your energy will be better used in a creative way. Just as the moon is always changing through its phases from nothing to fullness, so your emotions and physical energy may be fluctuating. The moon presides over a one month period of change. You may travel or move house during this time. You will need more rest than usual, to sleep, to dream, and to renew yourself. A change is certainly coming and may require all your energy.

Reversed Meaning

A period of indecision is ending. The time of fluctuations and change is over. You may move house or job, or you may simply move on from a muddled way of thinking. Confusions about true motives — yours or someone else's — will become crystal clear and you can act with certainty. You have more energy than you have had for a while, as though waking refreshed from a long sleep. There is a wisdom in the body which you can now fully heed. You know what you want and need, ranging from food, to company, to rest. Now able to be very true to yourself and others, you can express your love in direct and honest ways. All your feelings are much clearer, even the less pleasant ones. At least you are not in the dark any longer about how you feel. Your creativity is activated and you can start to make dreams into reality.

XIX.

The Sun

DESCRIPTION

The Sun card is filled with vivid, joyful images. The child, whose hair is garlanded with sunflowers and who rides a white horse, is the very picture of innocence and new life. Sunlight streaming, this card dawns with the promise of the new day. White animals are sacred in many cultures, and the horse is a creature that can carry us on its strong back. The child's arms are open wide as if to receive the joy of life. The child represents the Fool or the Innocent One, who is willing to enter into life without cynicism. Tall sunflowers remind us of the beauty of the True Self when allowed to grow. In the sky is a huge sun with 11 straight rays, and 10 curved rays corresponding to the 21 major cards with the boy as 0. The Fool. This card represents the optimism and joy of being our true selves.

XIX. The Sun

Upright Meaning

A time of darkness or doubt is behind you. The Sun is shining on your question bringing happiness, success, and self-fulfilment. You need to take the initiative now and begin to move towards your goals, whether personal, artistic, financial, romantic, or career-orientated. Just as the Sun lights up the sky, many matters that were hard to see or unclear will be revealed in the light of day. Some of these may have appeared more delightful or fanciful by candlelight or moonlight, but it is time to look directly to matters and act with decisiveness. You can take the lead regarding your question and you can seek help from those in authority who will be willing and able to assist you. If you have been feeling low in mind or body, the Sun will shine its healing rays upon your upturned face. Warmth will replace the cool of the night and you will feel your body and spirit rejuvenate.

A new optimism surrounds you as you feel somehow reborn, fresh, and new, like the young child in the card. There are protective and loving rays around you. The Sun rules the heart and the spine in the body, so you can act with a warm heart and feel the strength in your backbone as you stand up for yourself. The wall in the image represents the strength of accumulated wisdom, but the child has moved beyond the great traditions of our world and is simply itself, enjoying the moment. Such a state of bliss born from happily living in the *now*, is revered by mystics of many traditions. The Sun brings abundance, so you will have plenty for yourself and plenty to share with others. If your question relates to another, you will be treated generously and lovingly. Look at the open stance of the young child in the image and open yourself to the promise of new life and light.

XIX. The Sun

Reversed Meaning

The Sun seems to be shining on someone else and not you at present. This lack of light can lead to a lack of optimism in you or someone close to you. An emptiness echoes around your question as if something you once had or thought you had is gone. The Sun is a cyclic energy and the light will return, but you need to sustain faith and hope in the darkness. Do not dwell on what might seem to be a defeat regarding your query. You need your courage and determination to push on and to stay open to other options. When The Sun is reversed you need to fight the enemies of depression and narrow thinking; don't give in to defeatism. These destructive feelings can deaden your spirit and blind you to opportunities that may arise. Try to remain wide-eyed and curious. Connect to the joyful energy of the child within who finds utter joy in each moment and you can experience this heaven on earth.

XX.

Judgement

RULING PLANET: PLUTO

DESCRIPTION

An angel sounds her trumpet in the clouds above the people. The people below stand awakening to the call of the angel. We arise out of our old confined selves and experience something completely new. The angel teaches us about flying up and beyond the old structures we believed were real. A new reality is shown. In Medieval times the Judgement card was fearful, thought to depict the Judgement Day of which the Bible speaks. Older symbolism of the Judgement card is about rebirth, resurrection, and awakening to a new time, a new reality. The images of the card create an impression of an exciting call and a feeling of waking up to something exciting and new.

XX. Judgement

Upright Meaning

You have progressed in the area of your question and are now ready to be released into a new means of dealing with the matters at hand. As the image in the card suggests, you can hear a distant calling and are being awakened to a new stage of awareness. You are now more powerful than you have been in the past regarding your question. Now more balanced, you are released from old fears and obstacles. As you feel the release from these concerns, a whole way of being is beginning to emerge and you understand that a transformation is taking place. You feel lifted out of the old views you had about your area of inquiry, as if on unseen wings. The world looks different from this angel-eye view and different decisions can be made based on your new realizations. You will be given the grace of a different perspective.

You can now make decisions that may have proved difficult before, for many complex reasons. If you need to let go of someone or something this will now be possible, with gentleness and few regrets. You will be able to use your judgement wisely and base your decision on your own moral sense rather than being swayed or manipulated. Decisions are best made with a balance of reason and intuition at this time, but you will be aware that you are making a final decision about something. You can see your choices clearly. Rely on your own judgement and you will be fascinated by the changes that can happen now you are released from the old patterns. Health improves, a new job, new love, or a move is in the air. In fact, anything is possible now that you have surrendered and let go.

XX. Judgement

Reversed Meaning

When the Judgement card appears reversed, you may experience a sense of loss regarding your question. Negative emotions, guilt, shame, and self-reproach can surface over the way you have handled matters. You may feel that you have been punished for your inability to do better. However, you must resist the temptation to give up, to lose heart regarding the present issue. A decision needs to be made otherwise you may find yourself chasing an impossible dream or unattainable goal. Perhaps you heard the wrong trumpet or followed the wrong calling in the past. Now listen very carefully to your inner guide and also listen to the practical wisdom of others you trust. You can undo something that is worrying you. Let go the negativity regarding your self-worth. This release will bring forth the new life and growth which is trying to happen.

XXI.

The World

RULING PLANET: SATURN

DESCRIPTION

The World card depicts a goddess encircled by a wreath of leaves and beautiful fruits. This wreath is symbolic of the natural beginnings and endings in life, just as The World is the last card in the cycle of the Tarot Major Arcana. The goddess looks free and unencumbered by worries or concerns. In each corner of the card one of the symbols of the four fixed signs of the zodiac appears: an angel, a winged eagle, a winged cow, or a winged lion. These represent the fixed stars or unchanging principles which guard the Dance of Life. The mood or impression in the card is one of a carefree celebration of life. There is a sense of completion, and starting the new cycle afresh.

XXI. The World

Upright Meaning

The World card means that you have come full circle in the area of your query. You are now ready to step freely onto the new road, unencumbered by the past. The Tibetan Buddhists believe in the goddess Dakini, she who is the sky-goer, naked, ever-dancing, and ever-shifting, who opens the way to new and greater consciousness. The figure dancing in the middle of the oval-shaped wreath represents your completion of one cycle. Your rejoicing in the fresh and new is shown by the figure's nakedness. The oval or zero shape brings you back again to the Fool, who is called into life with innocence and a sense of adventure. Now, like the Fool, you face a whole new cycle, but this time you contain the wisdom of having already taken the journey through the spiritual learning of the Major Arcana. You are thus very well prepared for the next phase of your life.

The shape of the wreath resembles an egg, the matrix from which we all grow. Known as the Cosmic Egg, the symbol of wholeness and wisdom, it contains all the possibilities and hopes of a new life. So you are at the end and yet at the beginning in the area of your question. It is important to assess what baggage you want to take with you on the next part of the journey, as you will have to carry it for one whole cycle. It is best to travel light, both physically and emotionally. Indeed, you may be facing a period of expanding your horizons, maybe through travel. You have matured and are ready to take control of the chaos that is your life. Having earned the rewards that are now coming to you, personally or professionally, you are realistic and grounded. You are now ready to understand that true freedom comes from discipline, joy, and dedication to your own path. You are now ready to be designer, choreographer, and performer in your individual Dance of Life.

Reversed Meaning

The World reversed brings you to the end of a cycle, but there will be delays and frustration rather than a smooth transition. Uncomfortable as you may be about the changes that are taking place, you know deep within that an ending is upon you. You may experience a loss of momentum regarding your question. Things seem to be at a standstill and you can do nothing to speed up the outcome. However, you must resist the temptation to give up, or to lose your will regarding the present issue. A decision must be made, otherwise you may find yourself going round and round in circles. Your character is being tested and you must fight against inertia and stagnation. Let go of any rigidity in your mind around your question. You are on the brink of a new cycle so have faith, be flexible and patient. When the time is right, you will find the new road opens out before you.

Alternative Spreads

ALTERNATE PATHWAYS (2 CARD) SPREAD

Often we have an either/or question arise in our mind. "What would happen if I did X? What about if I did Y?" If you want to ask such a question it is simply a matter of holding the first option in your mind while washing the cards. Choose the first card and read the meaning from the Tarot Oracle. Repeat the procedure with the second part of your choice, placing the second card beside the first one.

Sample Interpretation — Tony

In one such question, Tony wanted to know whether he should pursue the option of working for himself, the card one option, or take up a well-paid job offer, the card two option. He drew The Fool reversed as card one and The Sun as card two. The Fool reversed warned him not to make any rash moves, that there may be some hidden snags in such a decision. It said that he did want to make a change but the time was not quite right for such a move. The Sun shone optimistically on option B, suggesting only good could come from such a decision.

PAST, PRESENT, FUTURE (3 CARD) SPREAD

One of the simplest alternative spreads is the Past, Present, Future spread. First wash the cards, then select card one to represent the past influences regarding your question. Place this card on your left. Select card two to describe present influences and place this card in front of you. Select a third card to represent the future trends of the matter in mind. Place this card to your right.

Suggested Reading

More general and historical information:
Douglas, Alfred, *The Tarot*, Arkana, London 1972

Gray, Eden, *A Complete Guide to the Tarot*, Bantam, New York 1972

Walker, Barbara G., *The Secrets of the Tarot*, Harper & Row, New York 1984

More on the Advanced Tarot and the Hebrew Cabala:
Lotterhand, Jason, *The Thursday Night Tarot*, Newcastle Publishing Co., California 1989

More on The Goddess:
Barker Woolger, Jennifer, and Woolger, Roger J., *The Goddess Within*, Rider, London 1990

More on Connecting to Intuition:
Estes, Clarissa Pinkola, *Women Who Run With the Wolves* , Rider, London 1992

The Feminine Perspective of Astrology:
River, Lindsay, and Gillespie, Sally, *The Knot of Time*, The Women's Press, London 1987 (Astrology)

More about Myth:
Sharman-Burke, Juliette, and Greene, Liz, *The Mythic Tarot*, Century Hutchinson Limited, London 1986